On a Safari

5, 10, 15

A Counting by Fives Book

by Martha E. H. Rustad

AMICUS READERS 1 AMICUS INK

amicus readers

Say Hello to Amicus Readers.

You'll find our helpful dog, Amicus, chasing a ball—to let you know the reading level of a book.

1

Learn to Read

High frequency words and close photo-text matches introduce familiar topics and provide ample support for brand new readers.

2

Read Independently

Some repetition is mixed with varied sentence structures and a select amount of new vocabulary words are introduced with text and photo support.

3

Read to Know More

Interesting facts and engaging art and photos give fluent readers fun books both for reading practice and to learn about new topics.

Amicus Readers and Amicus Ink are imprints of Amicus
P.O. Box 1329, Mankato, MN 56002
www.amicuspublishing.us

Library of Congress Cataloging-in-Publication Data
Names: Rustad, Martha E. H. (Martha Elizabeth Hillman), 1975- author.
Title: On a safari 5, 10, 15 : a counting by fives book / by Martha E. H. Rustad.
Description: Mankato, MN : Amicus, [2017] | Series: 1, 2, 3 count with me | Audience: K to grade 3.
Identifiers: LCCN 2015041513 (print) | LCCN 2015046554 (ebook) | ISBN 9781607539223 (library binding) | ISBN 9781681521138 (pbk.) | ISBN 9781681510460 (eBook)
Subjects: LCSH: Counting--Juvenile literature. | Animals--Africa--Juvenile literature.
Classification: LCC QA113 .R8936 2017 (print) | LCC QA113 (ebook) | DDC 513.2/11--dc23
LC record available at http://lccn.loc.gov/2015041513

Photo Credits: Alamy Stock Photo/MURILLO LARA MARIA LUISA, 1; Corbis Joseph Sohm/Visions of America, 3, Corbis/Suzi Eszterhas/Minden Pictures, 12; Dreamstime/Steffen Foerster, 13, Susan Robinson, 12, 13, 24, iStock/akinshin, 16, 17, 24, anankkml, 16, 17, 24, Antagain/16-17, Brian Raisbeck/cover, cyoginan, 18-19, DaddyBit, cover, EcoPic, 22-23, EdwardShackleford, 11, jez_bennett, 6, 7, nattanan726, 22-23, Nikola Nastasic, 16, 17, 24, olgysha2008, cover, tamsindove, 8, 9, 24, UroshPetrovic, cover; Shutterstock/Anan Kaewkhammul, 14-15, 20-21, Antonov Roman, 14-15, COLOMBO NICOLA, 20-21, Eric Isselee, 10, 11, GUDKOV ANDREY, 4, 5, konmesa, 22, 23, 24, Natalia Pushchina, 16-17, nutsiam, 14-15, prapass, 14-15, Tratong, 22-23, Vadim Nefedoff, 12

Editor   Rebecca Glaser
Designer   Tracy Myers

Printed in the United States of America

HC 10 9 8 7 6 5 4 3 2 1
PB 10 9 8 7 6 5 4 3 2 1

We can find lots of animals in Africa. Let's count by fives on a safari. Come along!

5

Five lions drink. A group of lions is called a pride. Roar!

Ten hippos cool off in the water.
They can hold their breath for
five minutes.

10

15

Fifteen elephants herd together.
They look for water.

20

Twenty wildebeests walk across the plains. They migrate to find food.

25

Twenty-five baboons sit on rocks. A group of baboons is called a troop.

30

Thirty zebras graze.

They chew hay and grasses.

Thirty-five giraffes eat leaves. Long necks reach tall trees.

35

Forty flamingos wade. They eat tiny water animals. Slurp!

40

45

Forty-five antelope watch for danger. They run fast if a lion comes!

Fifty meerkats look out of their holes. How many animals can you count?

50

Count Again

How many animals? Count by fives.